You Can Count on Me

I am responsible for all I do.

You can count on me.

I do my class work,

my homework, too.

I try to practice the golden rule.

I am responsible for all I do.

You can count on me.

I keep my promises to my friends.

I return the books the library lends.

I am responsible for all I do.

You can count on me.

I take care of the things friends loan.

I keep up with the things I own.

I am responsible for all I do.

You can count on me.